Thoughts to Leave Behind

Garris Elkins

Prophetic Horizons
Jacksonville, Oregon
United States

Thoughts to Leave Behind
© 2015 Garris Elkins

Prophetic Horizons
PO Box 509, Jacksonville, OR, 97530 USA
info@prophetichorizons.com | www.GarrisElkins.com

ISBN-13: 978-0692404218
ISBN-10: 069240421X

Dedication

To the Good Shepherd and all those who shepherd in His name. I offer this collection of thoughts to those who will follow my generation of leadership. May the ceiling of our greatest accomplishments become the floor of your new beginning.

"… and His faithfulness continues to each generation." –Psalm 100:5

Introduction

Recently, I concluded 33 years of pastoral ministry. We handed the church off to a faithful team of young leaders who will lead it into the future. While this process was taking place, I began to write down some thoughts I wanted to leave behind for our team and for others who might read these pages. These thoughts were birthed in the trenches of my experience as a pastor. Some of these thoughts are the result of my occasional success, but the majority I learned in the process of recovering from points of interpersonal challenges and personal brokenness.

The longer I have the privilege of serving God's people, the more I have come to realize the power of Spirit-guided insight. Points of insight are like a set of modern-day proverbs that can help steer us through our years of shepherding God's people. These concepts become the templates we place over the situations we encounter. From them we can make healthy adjustments to our personal lives and in the lives of those we care for.

I want this collection of thoughts to be a useful template. Read them to discover what might apply to your unique situation. My desire is that together we can pool our collective knowledge to better serve God's people with compassion and wisdom.

Wonder and Mystery

Make a place for wonder and mystery to always be present in your life and ministry. As you pastor a church, grow a family, or develop a business plan, there will be times when you find yourself falling into ruts of predictability. When you realize you have slipped into one of these ruts, call out to God to reveal to you a sense of wonder and mystery.

Life and ministry can too easily become predictable and lose a sense of adventure if we live within human reasoning alone. Developing a sense of wonder and mystery will help you believe that something bigger and unexplainable is taking place. Wonder and mystery are spiritual pry bars that will leverage you out of the ruts of predictability.

It is hard to explain wonder and mystery. A normal, everyday experience will lack the amazement that wonder produces. If you can explain what took place, it's not a mystery. The people you serve and the family you love are longing for something more. They want to encounter a God larger than the moment. Encourage people to never settle for a life experience void of these two energizing elements. Helping people contend for what is above and beyond what they could ever hope or dream for are the hallmarks of Spirit-led leadership.

Follow the Presence

There will be times in the coming years when you will run out of road. You will come to a place where you won't see the next step. In these moments, fear will try to take hold of your life and steer you toward the destination of despair.

When you begin to feel this way, remember: when you walk with God, you are never without an option. You carry the very presence of Jesus Christ.

While you carry His presence at all times, God can also choose to manifest His presence outside your life. The manifest presence of God will draw you forward to take steps of faith when no pathway is visible to the natural eye. This drawing of the Spirit is what the old timers called, "deep calling out to deep." Follow these inclinations. They will become your way forward.

Choose to Believe the Best

Choose to believe the best even when it seems like a worst-case scenario is developing. Believing the best is not putting your head in the sand or living a life of naivety. Believing the best is a way of living in hope all the way to the end, believing that something better is coming.

It is easy to give up too soon and to move on, thinking no good thing is possible. When a miracle eventually happens, our judgment and unbelief will put us in a place where we are unable to see the miracle that emerged from within the brokenness.

Choose to be the last person standing with broken people and broken situations. When you take this position and God does an eleventh-hour miracle, you can look into their eyes and say, "I always knew God was up to something good in your life." This is why faith is described as the substance of things not yet seen. Faith chooses to see the best when others only see the worst.

Trust Your Team

Every church, every family, and every business is a team. If you have done your job well, your team will know your heart and the things you are passionate about. You can trust them to make right decisions without having to manage every aspect of their lives and calling. This trust will release a deeper level of creativity within the team and allow each person to explore new levels of anointing.

When you need to make a decision that will affect the group, it is wise to give your team the time they need to process any proposed change. Do this before setting things in stone. A new vision can seem stark. Initial reactions are only that—reactions. Wait and trust. Include each team member in the process; not only will you be honoring them, their participation will show you things you cannot see.

There will be probably be a few emergencies where you need to make an on-the-spot decision, independent of feedback. When these rare moments come, you have permission to make those decisions. A healthy team will understand.

It is too easy to make decisions in a time of private frustration and then announce them publicly, bypassing team interaction. When this takes place, trust will begin to erode within the team. Your assignment is to release people to do their job with creativity and freedom. Trusting your team to do their job without hovering over them will allow them to rise to new levels in their calling and will keep you free to pray and dream about the future.

What Other People Think

You will have two opinions for every decision you make. Some people will like what you do, and others will not. Those who applaud you today may not do so tomorrow. Those who oppose you today could actually become co-laborers tomorrow.

Evaluate situations with patient wisdom. Before you make a decision, spend time with God and find out His heart for each situation you face. Wise leaders are led by revelation.

As your decisions become a reality and the differing opinions begin to spin around you, respond with humility and remain teachable. You can be vulnerable and open while still leading with strength and confidence. Humility will protect you.

Endings

Nothing is ever over until God says it is over. Never let people, a painful circumstance, or the devil define the end of anything.

When a situation seems dead and it feels like you are out of options, never forget one critical truth: with God, resurrection life is always present and possible. In the Kingdom of God, resurrection will ultimately be your ending.

You will encounter circumstances that look like death more than once: the death of a dream, a relationship, or a ministry. You can't prepare for these future events apart from learning to trust God today.

In times that feel like death, your only option will be to trust in God's faithfulness to raise you up—just like Jesus did when He lay in the tomb awaiting His resurrection. God will be faithful. He promises to raise dead things to new life.

Be the First to Forgive

As you walk through life, you will collide with people. When this happens, and you get wounded, be the first to forgive. Forgiveness needs to be granted early. The longer the gap of time between the offense and the resolution of the offense, the greater the chance the enemy has to get a foothold in your heart.

Being the first to forgive means you are large enough in spirit to lay down your rights, your demand to be treated fairly, and the unmet expectations of what you think should have happened. These three issues belong on the Cross in a place of permanent death because waiting for others to uphold your rights and treat you fairly or meet your expectations are impossible requirements to put on another person.

Act now to make things right, and experience the freedom of being the first to forgive. Your act of forgiveness will help you cross the threshold of a doorway that will lead you to your destiny.

The Hidden Reef of Self-Pity

There is a reef hidden under the surface of your life journey. It is called self-pity. Self-pity remains hidden away like an uncharted coral reef. It is hard to detect and easy to strike if not recognized with honesty. Self-pity says things like: "I always need to be treated fairly." "I always need to be understood." "I always need to be accepted."

This "I-always-need" attitude is really a demand we make of God and others when the grind of life has left us feeling alone. We want the pain to go away, but we don't know how to make that happen. In these times, self-pity invites us to make a subtle course adjustment to align our thinking with the direction of its lie. Capsizing and eventual disaster await all who continue to sail this course.

God has always been with you. Never allow self-pity to linger in your thoughts, convincing you that you are alone and no one understands your plight. Self-pity is a stowaway who possesses a false set of navigational charts that will be offered to you in times of conflict and depression. Throw this imposter overboard. This is a task only you can do. Once you recognize and renounce this mindset, you will be free to sail forward without fear into the deep waters of the Spirit.

The Weakness of Your Strength

There can be a problem with having confidence in the strength of our giftings and talents. Eventually, these strengths can become some of the greatest barriers to the work of God. Living and ministering from your own strength creates a false confidence, causing you to believe you can accomplish the will of God apart from the power of God.

Jesus said to Paul, "My grace is all you need. My power works best in weakness." Paul's response to the words of the Lord was delight—he said, "So now I am glad." Paul also said, "For when I am weak, then I am strong."

Over the years, you will be told to develop the areas of your greatest strengths. This is just the opposite of what Jesus asks of you. He would say, "Develop the place of your greatest weakness. This is the place where I will do my greatest work in you." I think the Lord would say this because in those places where you feel the weakest, God will not have to deal with the barrier of your pride when He approaches your life with an offer of wholeness.

It will be in these places of restored brokenness that God will reveal your destiny and fulfill your calling. If you let God develop your weak places, you will be able to say, like Paul, "So now I am glad to boast about my weaknesses, so that the power of Christ can work through me."

Spiritual Janitors

You have not been called to always be a spiritual janitor. All the messes caused by other people are not immediately your concern. Your rush to clean things up could actually get in the way of what God wants to do. Be careful you don't create in others the need for your presence to resolve each and every conflict in their life. You may feel needed, but in the end, you will actually be robbing others of their responsibility to call on the Lord instead of calling on you. Transformation occurs from within the messes of life.

We are asked to bear the burdens of others, but we have not been given permission to take on the weight of their choices. Jesus said that anything we carry in His name would be light and not cumbersome. This includes the burdens of others. Jesus never asked you to bear the weight of another person's poor decision-making process. When you begin to carry this weight, the relationship will get heavy and clumsy with a responsibility that is not yours. That weight will be your clue that you have assumed a role you were never assigned or designed to fulfill.

Take Your Spouse with You

Life is a journey. If you are married, the journey includes two people — not one. The image of isolated prophets who "hear God" and then drag their spouse forward in reluctance is not the image of a healthy relationship.

A wise pastor once told me, "The real test of your leadership will come many years from now when we look at your wife. If she still has a beautiful soul and is growing in that beauty, you will have become a good leader." That same person also said, "Ask your wife what she wants to do. What is her passion? These are her decisions, not decisions other people should make for her. Spend the rest of your life together learning how to support her decision."

Neither spouse has to be what other people demand of them — they can simply become the person God has called them to be. The discovery of this freedom is dangerous to the kingdom of darkness. When you choose to include your spouse and invite them to walk alongside you in their unique, God-assigned path, you will find 10,000 fleeing before you as a couple when on your best day as a solo act you could only frighten 1,000.

The Breakthrough of Blessing

At many points of opposition and resistance on your journey of faith, you will discover the way forward when you choose to step through the doorway of blessing. Forgiving and choosing to bless those who oppose you will keep your heart tender and open to the Lord. Your blessing, once released, becomes a miraculous point of breakthrough for you and for those who stand in opposition to you.

When you are faced with misunderstanding, rejection, or unforgiving attitudes, your way forward will be revealed on the other side of your ability to bless those who oppose you. These supernatural doorways only appear to those who are willing to let go of the controlling power of pain and sorrow. Bless your enemies, and forgive your transgressors. This is the way of Jesus and the way forward for those who have discovered His heart.

Avoid Early Criticism

Make the choice to not align with the first critical voices demanding your agreement with their narrow interpretation of the facts. Many times, the first response to an issue is premature and uninformed. If you join in with this initial, knee-jerk, crowd reaction, you will allow the emotions of others to define you and your voice. Give yourself the time needed to allow the Lord to speak to you before you choose to speak for Him. Let God's heart—not your emotions—craft your response.

The word the Lord gives to you might actually go against the established party line. This will require another level of wisdom—the wisdom of knowing when to speak into the fervor of an excited crowd. Some have spoken too early, and others have spoken too late. The missed timing of a word from God can diminish the impact of what He asked you to share.

Having a word from God is critical in order to wisely navigate through intense times of cultural change. Just as critical as the word is the timing and delivery of that word. The writer of Proverbs said, "Timely advice is lovely, like golden apples in a silver basket" (Proverbs 25:11).

Arguing in Absence

One of the most devastating things you can do is to allow an argument to take place in your mind when the other person is not present. These one-sided arguments happen when you provide both sides of the conversation. Unresolved mental disputes will eventually result in suspicion and separation from the very people God has brought into your life. Darkness extends these invitations to us, and — unless we confront them — they will eventually do great damage within the Church.

The Scriptures tell us to take our thoughts captive and make them obedient to Jesus Christ. Arrest and handcuff errant thoughts before they are allowed to sow their devastating results. This is accomplished by choosing to respond in the opposite spirit. Fighting and getting drawn into the fray while becoming defensive will only cause more conflict.

Lay down the demand that other people treat you fairly within your definition of justice. Choose to receive what only God can give. He is truth, and He alone is justice.

Just Show Up

Some of the greatest things in life happen when you simply choose to show up in a place of expected responsibility. Choose to show up when you don't want to. Choose to show up on time. Choose to show up in places of righteous expectation. Choose to show up emotionally as a parent or spouse. Simply choosing to show up is a beautiful expression of God's heart in human form.

Showing up is about the power of presence. You carry the very presence of God. Your arrival with God will displace many things that would run rampant had you been absent.

You never arrive in a situation alone—even when no one else shows up. You will always arrive with God. The two of you can challenge any lie and defeat its power by simply showing up together.

Possessing Unexplainable Peace

Scripture tells us a peace is available that exceeds anything we can understand. This kind of peace is available even when what is causing our lack of peace is still present and active in our life. This is a God-peace that comes in the middle of the turmoil and simply rests upon our life as a gift despite what is happening around us.

This peace doesn't come because at some point we finally understood why everything took place that has made our lives so unsettling. Understanding our present reality does not and cannot bring this peace. This is why we are told that we experience the peace of God in a place beyond our ability to understand its presence in our lives; it simply comes to us.

We discover this peace when we are willing to exchange a state of anxiety for a prayer of thankfulness: a prayer offered from within our current conflict. Once this exchange is made, it will become an invitation that ushers in the peace we are seeking.

Every Ending Is a Beginning

For every ending—the end of a relationship, a ministry, a dream—there exists a new beginning. These unexpected endings can be forced upon you by a life circumstance or by your own poor choices. God can use them as vehicles to take you into a new and hope-filled future fully known by Him, but unexplored by you.

Resist the invitation to return to old patterns of life and unbelief offered by those who do not believe in your new future. Those old ways of thinking may have contributed to things falling apart in the first place. You are hungry for a fresh start. Feed that hunger with a feast of God's presence. His presence will be your source of strength and nourishment for the coming journey into your new beginning.

The Power of Expectancy

Throughout history, when there existed in the people of God an expectancy that something supernatural could take place at any moment, the manifestation of God's presence appeared in the form of signs, wonders, and miracles. The thief of our hope comes to steal this expectancy when we make the choice to yield to the status quo and call it our reality.

There is a solution for this dilemma. The solution is to look. The essence of faith is to look at the substance of heaven not yet revealed on earth. This act of looking with faith sees past the veil that separates the status quo of time and space and sees the plans of heaven. The substance of this heavenly insight is what we bring back into our current circumstance and what we use to begin living a life of expectancy. When this transaction takes place, our faith will reposition our lives and attitudes to experience on earth what was first seen in heaven. This is the power of expectancy.

Healthy Life Transitions

I have noticed a common denominator in every successful life transition. Those who were able to navigate through times of change and come out on the other side emotionally and spiritually healthy understood one profound truth: God is good, and He is always leading us to a good place. Without knowing that the goodness of God awaits us at each step in the journey, fear will eventually come and immobilize us and those making the transition with us.

An understanding of God's goodness has the power to direct every aspect of a transition. Before you step forward, make sure you have settled this issue. The knowledge of God's goodness will be your only safe compass for the journey.

If It's Not Broken

Someone once said, "If it's not broken, don't fix it." This might apply to cars and machinery but not necessarily to advancing the Kingdom of God on earth. As the revelation of Jesus Christ continues to expand, each new season will require a reexamination of how effective our current model of the Church really is at accomplishing the will of God.

We need to remain open to personal and corporate course corrections at all points along our journey. If we want to be a healthy follower of Christ, we will welcome — and sometimes struggle with — these needed course corrections. These corrections will help us see whether we have mentally or emotionally put our lives and ministries on a form of spiritual autopilot, assuming that what worked in the past will continue to work in the future. Expansion, increase, and new life will always require change and adjustment for the Church to move beyond a current "relevancy" into a place of supernatural manifestation and advancement.

Life Near the Edge

I was raised by parents who lived through the pain and lack of the Great Depression. My father had to hop the rails for nine years looking for work and food. My mother was part of a divorced family who struggled to make ends meet in the segregated South of the 1930's after my grandfather left for work one day and never returned.

My grandmother ran a boarding house while my mother ran barefoot along the dirt streets of her hometown in Alexandria, Louisiana. Like many others who grew up in the poverty of the Depression, my parents made sure their children would never suffer as they did. Growing up, I never missed a meal or lacked anything.

Over the years, I have come to realize that people who live the closest to the edge of anything have formed a theology of life the rest of us miss growing up in a lifestyle where every need has a solution. Some of us failed to accumulate these life skills of discernment because we have lived within the cushioned illusion of possessions, a never-ending supply of everything, and an over-confidence in self. These illusions are created in Western cultures where hunger does not normally visit our home, and terror happens elsewhere.

A theology of life crafted in the insulated comfort of a local coffee shop will lack the depth of reality needed to address the real issues of life. Craft your response to the poor by sharing the meal they are forced to eat. Develop your concept of Christian pacifism while imagining that extreme violence is knocking at your door. Draft your theology of God's mercy when you have suffered your greatest failure. These are the places where honest answers are discovered and where the credibility of our faith is established.

Pursuing Excellence

The word "excellence" in the language of the New Testament has been translated in several ways. It can mean "goodness," "the manifestation of God's power," or "a miracle."

In our pursuit of excellence within the Church, we should never allow excellence to only mean clean floors, hip video productions, or the finely measured elements of a well-planned worship service.

Experiencing the excellence of God is the result of making room for His presence when we gather. The plans that flow from that kind of expectation will make possible the release of His goodness, power, and miracles. That kind of gathering will define what is truly excellent.

Managers and Apostles

The difference between an organization and a movement is found in the style of its leadership. There are two kinds of leaders: managers and apostles. Both are gifted and called to fulfill specific assignments within the Church.

A manager is particularly gifted in making sure the essential care is provided for a group to prosper. However, without an apostolic voice, managers can become overly protective while maintaining the status quo. If left unchallenged, they will manage an organization to a standstill and eventual death. Managers can get nervous at the sound of an apostolic voice because an apostle leads by revelation, and revelation has the potential to challenge the managed status of an organization.

A manager can view apostolic initiative as a threat to the system. This perceived threat could cause a manager to try and gain more control by removing the apostolic voice from the organizational process. An apostolic gift is assigned by the Lord to confront, with honor, the restrictions and ways of thinking found in an organization that are currently producing its eventual decline and demise.

Apostles initiate change by inviting and releasing

those with a similar apostolic calling to move forward at the speed of their faith into new areas of ministry potential, thereby creating the forward motion inherent in a movement.

Laying Down Your Painful History

There are times when two people will experience something so challenging that in order to move forward, each of them will need to agree to lay down their shared history without demanding anything from the other person. This is not ignoring what took place; rather, it is realizing that a confusing past can be too intertwined and bound up in mutual pain to be separated. Only God can unravel some things.

After you lay down your history, God will someday bring up the hurtful things that took place. He does so because not dealing with this part of your history will eventually inhibit your forward progress. God doesn't do this to punish you or the other person. He never shames His children into obedience. He brings things to light to begin the process of unraveling a confusing past and to give you the hope of a final and personal resolution.

God will be able to do this because in the process of healing, you will have experienced a new level of humility that comes from recognizing your own need and allowing God to transform your life. You will know your personal healing has begun when you find yourself pursuing the will of God more than pursuing your need to have things work out the way you had planned.

Accelerated Maturity

Your spiritual maturity is not based on chronological time spent in a religious group. Your history does not mature you. Living a certain number of years does not make a person wiser or more loving. Gray hair is not a guarantee of wisdom. Spiritual maturity is measured by the length of time between the realization of your sin and your willingness to repent. The shorter the duration of this cycle—void of delaying excuses and justifications—is what defines a mature person.

God is poised and ready to accelerate your life, but He first needs from you a willing and pliable heart in order to bring increase. Take time each day to wait and be still. Listen to the Holy Spirit. Be purposeful about dealing with any sin that comes to mind in this waiting.

As you choose to live this kind of yielded life, you will find yourself arriving in places of spiritual maturity you had previously thought impossible. Every area of your life that you allow God to transform will become the place of your greatest personal freedom. You will then be able to give God the glory for something only His grace could have made possible. This will become your testimony.

Kingdom Prayers

Kingdom prayer is noticeably different than a prayer fueled only by sorrow and fear. Kingdom prayer sees past the natural headlines of wars and rumors of wars and looks into the heart of God. Kingdom prayer invites the promises of God to invade the earth. It petitions breakthrough. This kind of prayer declares God's preferred future for individuals, families and nations.

Kingdom prayer will sound different because it does not wring its hands when faced with momentary affliction. It sees victory when others only see defeat. Kingdom prayer declares, decrees, and commands that the powers on earth yield to the authority of heaven. Those who learn to pray this way are able to wait with patience for the breakthrough this kind of prayer anticipates.

When the Bottom Falls Out

There are events in life that will leave you feeling like the floor has fallen out from beneath your feet. Your place of stability will feel like it disappeared. What was once a secure platform can give way like a trap door and cause you to feel like you are in an emotional free fall.

At first you will feel panic. An unplanned and unexpected falling is a fearful thing to experience. Because God promised to never leave you or forsake you, there is always the promise of a sure and solid place for your feet to land once this free-fall season comes to an end. With God you will always land on your feet knowing He is holding you as you entrust yourself to Him.

As you fall, you will need to make the choice to worship God for His love and for His goodness. This is the only way you will be able to keep your wits about you until God brings a resolution.

This kind of worship is not based on your circumstance but solely on the heart of God. Your act of worship will guide your feet to finally land upon a solid place that waits for you in your future.

God will use these uncomfortable experiences to take

you deeper into your understanding of His love. That will be your ultimate destination once a season of falling is complete.

This Wall of Judgment

A wall of judgment can spring up in front of you without warning. A comment someone makes can cause this wall to appear, and its presence has the ability to impede your forward motion if not challenged. It is strange how one comment can so completely derail how you feel and bring life to a sudden stop.

These comments are not the real problem—neither is your reaction. Your reaction will help you see where the real problem is located. Sight is the beginning of healing. The hidden root issue that triggers our reaction is the real issue, and these issues can be hidden beneath layers of life experience. These root problems must first be seen and identified before a true and lasting healing can begin to take place.

Follow the fruit of your response down through the branches and limbs of your feelings, through the trunk of your being into to the lowest place in your emotional root structure where your thoughts will reveal your beliefs. It will be in this deepest place, hidden beneath life's gritty relational soil, that you will discover the lie that awaits the clipping shears of truth.

As you prune away this lie, a new level of confidence

in God will rise up, and your life will begin to bear the fruit of truth that has the power to dismantle a wall of judgment.

Pioneering a New Season in Your Life

Years ago, when Jan and I ventured out to start our first church, those who sent us described church planters as people who would "pioneer" a new church. That word is not used very much in church-planting circles today, but it remains accurate in describing our assignment. We packed up all our belongings, along with our two young children and two cats. We drove 750 miles into the unknown, holding only a promise from God. That is the nature of a pioneer.

In the settling of the American West, those who rode in wagons and walked alongside them toward the hope of a new beginning were called pioneers. The dictionary defines a pioneer as "one who ventures into unknown or unclaimed territory." This has a larger application than just historic pioneers or present-day church planters. This definition describes each life that steps away from what is known and travels forward into the expanse of an unexplored future.

You may find yourself at the end of a known season. What lies before you is an unexplored landscape that contains a promise from God of something not yet seen with the natural eye. A pioneer sees this invisible place with the eyes of faith.

You can stay where you are, but you will always live with the lingering question, "What would have happened if we had made the journey?" If this is where you find yourself, ask God to give you the heart of a pioneer. You will know when this happens because the hope of the promise will have overshadowed the doubt of your pending departure. You will find yourself packing with expectancy for a new adventure experienced only by those who have the heart of a pioneer.

Until I Get There

I have been a pastor for many years. I am now seen as a spiritual father. This is a high calling and one I hope to carry with honor the rest of my days. As a spiritual father, I want to make sure my sons and daughters finish well so that some day they will also have the honor of becoming a spiritual father or mother.

When Paul wrote his two letters to Timothy, he was writing to a young leader who was struggling. From the content of Paul's letters, it was evident that Timothy needed to stir up the gifts previously planted in his life. Timothy may have been trying to do ministry out of his own strength—something we all have done from time to time. Paul gave Timothy a simple instruction found in I Timothy 4:13: "Until I get there, focus on reading the Scriptures to the church, encouraging the believers, and teaching them." This was Paul's fatherly advice for Timothy until Paul could arrive and help him sort things out.

If you lead a ministry, whether a church, a small group, your family, or a large denomination, this advice also applies to you. This is especially important in those times when you are tired from trying to do ministry in your own strength or under the burden of other people's expectations. Call for your spiritual father or mother to come and spend time with you. Until they arrive, chose to get simple once again. Stir up the gifts that were placed in you in the beginning. When you gather with those under your care, read the Word, encourage people and teach them the way of faith. This is the kind of simple life God loves to visit with a fresh outpouring of power.

Honor Is a Weapon

Honor is a weapon that can destroy the plans and strategies of hell. When you give honor to people — to the guilty and the innocent alike — something supernatural is released.

To a mind limited by natural thinking, honor must first be earned. Those who require you to earn their honor will only grant it after you have aligned with their demands. Honor cannot be demanded. It is not the product of alignment. When God grants honor, He gives it freely before it can be earned.

The moment you were born again, you were placed in Christ where He now sits in a place of honor at the right hand of the Father. You are also sitting with Him in that place of honor even while you still struggle with certain aspects of your life here on earth.

Your struggle does not cancel God's gift of honor. The Father honored the Son by putting all things under His feet, and ultimately, under your feet. All things that stand in opposition to God's love in your life will eventually bow before you in defeat as you thrust the weapon of honor into the heart of dishonor whenever it rears its head.

Let People Tell Their Own Story

It is too easy to want to tell the story of another person's life, especially when your relationship has been a challenge. Resist this urge—especially when the story you are telling is about the life of someone who has hurt or wounded you.

Our storytelling of another person's life can devolve into defending our part in a broken relationship. These stories can become a defense for our actions and will not share the full scope of what took place because the other person is not present to share their perspective.

When these opportunities to craft a biased narrative come, resist them. Instead, craft words filled with hope and blessing for the other person. As you share, be willing to admit you may have contributed to the breakdown of the relationship. This restrained and honest response will create trust in your hearers and trust in the hearts of those with whom you have a broken relationship. Give this process enough time, and God will be able to use your words of honor to build a bridge that will someday span the pain of the past and extend an invitation to a future of restoration.

The Endorsement of Your Ministry

The endorsement of your life and ministry takes place when the supernatural presence of Jesus is made known. This is what Peter described on the Day of Pentecost when he told those assembled, "God publicly endorsed Jesus the Nazarene by doing powerful miracles, wonders and signs through him, as you well know." The result of this endorsement — when God makes His miraculous presence known — is where the deepest and most culturally transforming events take place.

Revisit your priorities from time to time to make sure you have not reduced your life down to only doing good works in God's name. It is too easy to slip into a form of ministry that ceases to contend for the supernatural things Peter described on the Day of Pentecost.

The good works you are doing are important, but they are limited in their ability to impact culture. Good works are only vehicles used to bring you face to face with human need. It is at this point of contact with human need where you will have the opportunity to call for the power of God to come and do things that good works alone can never accomplish. Your invitation will allow Jesus to come and endorse His supernatural presence in your life.

This is the best endorsement you will ever receive.

Position Yourself Wisely

A wise man once told me he never wanted to take a position where he would be required to represent an organization to people. He always wanted to be in a position to represent people to the organization. Finding this position requires wisdom. Where you stand will determine whom you represent.

You are a representative of Jesus no matter where you serve. Your assignment, in whatever system or structure you find yourself, is where you have been called to represent the heart of God.

Don't get so caught up in the mechanics of any organization that your position would require you to draw your life and identity from the system. No matter where you go within your unique circle of relationships, make sure your brand loyalty remains with Jesus — not the perpetuation of the system. This will give your voice a power and credibility that only comes from knowing where you stand.

Religious Skeletons

Our physical body is supported by our skeletal structure. Remove our skeleton, and we would fall to the floor in an unrecognizable mass of tissue. The same is true for any group or institution. We need some form of structure to support life.

As with a healthy physical body, the skeleton should not be the first thing we notice when we meet someone. Tragic death camp pictures of starving people, where human beings were reduced to walking skeletons, is how a group or institution can appear if too much emphasis is placed on structure instead of the life the structure supports. You will need a basic structure as a support mechanism for the life God is birthing in your calling, but keep it to a minimum.

The Early Church saw how important this minimalist approach was in Acts 15 as the Gentile Church was being birthed beyond Jerusalem. Wise leaders suggested they should only ask a few things of these new Gentile believers while those in Jerusalem would have imposed their law and customs on the young Gentile Church. Instead, what happened was the birth of a healthy image of a church in its unique cultural context. Because of this wise decision, a skeletal structure was not the first thing noticed when the Gentile believers greeted their host culture with the new and life-giving message of Jesus Christ.

Outwitting Your Imposter

Inside each of us lives an imposter. This imposter wants to ruin your life by leading you away from the person God created you to be by having you assume a false identity. You have to learn to outwit the imposter. This outwitting is done with truth, honor, and the knowledge of your true identity.

Truth creates brutally honest conversations. Talk to yourself—the new one, the real one—and ask that person to take over the conversation with the imposter. As you begin to speak truth, honor will come forth because honor is the product of truth.

With God, nothing is ever lost—even in the times when you walked away with the imposter believing a lie. The good work God has done in you simply gets misplaced in the confusing seasons of life. Honor will reach out and recapture the real you, dust off the neglect and abuse that took place, and point you in the right direction once again. The Prodigal Son learned this lesson when he returned home and the Father restored his life. Your identity was never in jeopardy. You are seated in Christ at the right hand of the Father, safe and secure in heaven, apart from the broken seasons of your life.

The imposter will try to tell you lies, dishonor your life, and falsify the new creation you have become. Refuse to be a victim. Call him out. Fight him in a spiritual, bare-knuckle brawl, and reset your boundaries. This fight will go on in different forms for the rest of your life. Paul told the Galatians there is never a time when these two identities are not in conflict with each other. Don't let that thought trouble you. It is the stuff of real life in the Spirit.

Choose Your Battles Wisely

Twenty-five years ago, I asked a wise pastor his opinion about the battles he fought over issues of faith. As a young pastor, he had been known to pick verbal fights with anyone who disagreed with him. He had thankfully mellowed over the years.

I asked this pastor to describe the most important life lesson he had learned. He said, "I have learned to exercise more wisdom in the battles I choose to fight." In other words, he only entered battles that had eternal consequence. The rest of the battles were over personal opinion and interpretation of non-essential issues, and none of those battles were worth shedding relational blood over.

The Apostle Paul said, "Accept other believers...and don't argue with them about what they think is right or wrong" (Romans 14:1). If our lives are going to model the oneness that Paul described, we need to accept each other with open arms and honest conversation and not step into battles that don't need to be fought.

Living Aware

An understanding exists among those who teach self-defense that there are three kinds of people: sheep, wolves, and sheep dogs. Sheep are the vast majority of people in our culture—in the Church and out of it—who are absolutely unaware of the dangers that surround them. Wolves prey on this naïveté and lack of awareness. And then there are the sheep dogs who put themselves between the sheep and the hungry wolves to protect the sheep.

As the Church, we are called to put ourselves between people and the threats of darkness that seek to devour them. This requires that we actually recognize the threat and develop a plan of offense against the aggressor. We confront wolves with weapons powerful enough to bring down the most elaborate plans of darkness. This is an aggressive form of spiritual warfare much like David confronting Goliath.

Years ago a wise pastor told me, "You don't convert wolves—you shoot them!" To most sheep, this could sound harsh, but in reality it is an act of love. He was addressing a wolfing spirit that will only back down from devouring the flock if it is confronted with truth in the authority and power of Jesus Christ.

This confrontation can take place with a stealthy prayer offered in the middle of the night, an act of kindness to an unloving recipient, or the granting of forgiveness when we would rather hold a grudge. Because sheep have very little situational awareness, they may not even know you are there, standing between them and a hungry wolf that sees them only as prey. Your participation with the Spirit of God will dismantle the attack strategy of darkness and give a sheep the time and training needed to become a sheep dog.

Spiritual Traction

Traction is different than momentum. Traction gets your wheels moving and helps you sustain forward motion. Momentum is gained during traction, but it is only maintained if traction continues to be supplied to the wheels.

It is too easy to live off of the momentum produced in a previous season. There is an accompanying illusion that wants you to believe your current momentum can be sustained indefinitely. Spiritual traction is produced when you live in a moment-by-moment dependence on God. This kind of traction is required if you are going to move forward into the place of greater revelation God has destined for you.

Your current momentum will eventually play out and leave you stalled on the roadside if you try to move forward without inquiring of God. Reengage the gears of your spiritual life, and a fresh word of traction will come. Obey this word, and you will hear the screech of your spiritual tires as they once again take hold, producing traction and a renewed forward momentum for the next leg of your journey.

Slippery Slopes

There are slippery slopes on both sides of every mountain of human opinion. Be careful. Some people believe that slippery slopes exist only on the opposite side of the mountain from their current understanding of the facts.

When you ask God for wisdom, you are not asking Him to confirm your opinion. Your request for wisdom is an invitation for the Spirit to come and make adjustments in your thinking before you begin to communicate with others.

It will be in this reception of God's wisdom and the subsequent adjustments to your thinking where humility and mercy will begin to flow through you to those who hold a differing opinion. Humility and mercy are the evidence that you have received wisdom from above. This evidence is the only true foothold on the mountain of public opinion.

When Love Requires That You Move On

Don't allow another person's bewilderment to become your reality. Just because someone cannot understand your choices doesn't mean you can allow their misunderstanding to hinder you from moving forward in obedience to God.

There are times when love requires that you leave some people behind. This can seem cruel and uncaring, but it is an expression of love. Some people wanted Jesus to stay and not go to the Cross, but He chose to keep moving forward because His love was expressed in obedience.

Before you start this journey, make sure it is God who is asking you to move on. Don't make your decision because you have become impatient with your life and how it is developing. When God speaks instruction, He will be faithful to empower and direct your steps as you move forward in obedience. His word will become your only comfort when the questions and the doubts come to visit.

At some point, the protests of those who disagree with your choice will become only distant and indiscernible sounds of a past to which you are no longer connected.

Hanging out Together on Purpose

During the last several decades, the Church in Western culture has become over-programmed. I think we educated ourselves into this predicament. There now exists a program for almost everything — including discipleship. But that is changing. A new generation of people is emerging — young and old alike — who love God and His Church so much they are unwilling to settle for anything less than a return to something simple.

I have been a pastor for almost 35 years. I became a believer when I was a young boy. I have never attended a single class on discipleship. Frankly, because of my understanding of relational discipleship, I wouldn't even know how to teach on the subject. I don't want to negate study and training, but when discipleship becomes only an academic topic transmitted through an educational process, it loses some of its original intent.

My initial imprint on the subject came years ago when I heard a wise leader say, "Discipleship is never taught — it is caught. Discipleship is hanging out together on purpose." This sounds like something Jesus would say. For three years, He walked, lived, ate, and shared life with 12 people. This relationship was not accomplished with programs but with His presence. It was in the presence of Jesus where His first followers experienced life together and where the miracle of becoming a disciple took place. It is a miracle because it is a Spirit-generated process of transformation that takes place during an encounter with the Living Word Himself.

The Pause Before You Respond

Before you respond to a question or enter a conversation, you should always give yourself a moment to pause and collect your thoughts. This pause gives the Spirit time to speak to you.

Be careful: there is more than one kind of pause. For one kind pause, you craft your response from fear of what others in the group will think of your answer. Decisions that come from this kind of pause lack courage and value group acceptance over truth.

The other kind of pause waits to hear what the Spirit is saying and then wisely crafts a response by speaking the truth in love no matter what the cost. This response does not create answers based on what the group wants to hear but only on what the Spirit wants to say.

The next time you are asked for your opinion, examine what takes place in the pause. If you find you are responding out of fear, ask God to heal you before you respond. God wants to transform you into someone He can trust to give a courageous answer to the most challenging questions of life. He wants to do this because He has some important things to say through you.

The Legacy You Leave Behind

As you grow older, you will begin to think about the legacy you will leave behind. Many people who pursue a legacy of accomplishments and notoriety end up tired, bitter, and alone. God wants you to discover another kind of legacy that has a far greater impact on those who will follow in your footsteps.

The only legacy that has a lasting impact is the one that testifies to the faithfulness of God. God's faithfulness is the testimony of your life while you are living, and it can become the legacy of your life once you are gone. Anything less will not have the substance to endure.

In your history is the record of God's faithfulness. This is the legacy of His goodness that you have experienced in every season and in every situation of life. Living a life formed around this understanding is what changed you over time, and it will be what changes the lives of those who follow the example of your life long after your time on earth is complete.

Choose Wisely

Some of the goodness you are now experiencing can be traced back to a single decision someone made years ago A decision was made to believe for more, and that choice has become a blessing in your life. God began to position His promise around that single decision for its fulfillment somewhere in your future.

Your current circle of relationships and alliances were all positioned to intersect in your life today because of decisions made long ago. Your decisions can help create a future and release a destiny for people currently in your life and for those you do not yet know.

The most seemingly insignificant decision you make today has tremendous potential both now and in the future. It can become too easy to think some of these less prominent decisions—the ones without lots of fanfare—have little consequence. No decision is without power and consequence. Future generations will trace their blessing back to you and the decisions you make today. Choose wisely.

Horizontal Leadership Structures

The most prominent form of leadership structure is vertical. This form of leadership resembles a totem pole. The leader on top must leave, die, or be removed in order to make room for those waiting below who want to rise higher.

The totem pole advances its mission by addition—adding to the bottom to create vertical increase. But by increasing its height, this structure becomes relationally unstable. The higher one rises, the more distant you become from those you need the most.

A horizontal model of leadership is different. This model lays the totem pole structure down on its side and allows each member of the team to have their boots on the ground moving forward at different speeds based on their unique gifts and calling. The horizontal model is stable and moves forward by multiplication.

An apostolic structure is not hierarchal or vertical. In the horizontal structure, apostles stand side by side with other equipping gifts. Apostles are first off the line once the leadership model is brought down to earth. These sent ones simply move out ahead of the rest of the team to explore new spiritual territory.

As your leadership team chooses to lay down a vertical organizational structure, the results of the newly adopted horizontal model will begin to multiply supernaturally, releasing the untapped potential of your team.

Two Kinds of Whispers

There are two kinds of whispers. One is spoken behind your back. This whisper is demeaning and dishonoring. The other whisper the whisper of God — is spoken directly to you, face to face. The whispers of God affirm and encourage.

God's whispers of hope are always out in front of you, inviting you to something good and new. God will only have you visit your past to set you free from its failure and bondage so you can begin to move forward once again.

You can never stop these behind-the-back whisperers. They want to turn you around and away from the future to focus only on the past. Turn back around and look forward; this is where the face of God is positioned, speaking words of affirmation and inviting you to the hope of something new.

You Threw in the Towel Too Early

The phrase "throwing in the towel" was used in boxing matches when the trainer saw that his boxer was getting destroyed in the ring. The trainer, seeing what appeared to be an inevitable and devastating defeat, would throw a towel into the ring, and the referee would stop the fight.

There will come a challenging season when you will throw in the towel. You will think it's all over, and defeat will be the only epitaph for what took place. God has another plan.

God will ask you to walk back into the ring and retrieve your towel. God did not say it was over—you made that decision. You felt it was over because you were tired of watching the bloody fight, and you were weary from all the drama.

As you humbly walk back into the ring and pick up the towel you tossed in a moment of frustration, God will do something powerful in your heart. Your entry into the ring will be a visible admission that you walked away too soon. Your act of humble obedience will give others who have also quit too early the courage to try again. Your example will help them reengage their personal battles and understand that only God can say when something is truly over.

Invisible Doorways

The way forward you seek is through the doorway of faith. What is on the other side will remain invisible until you step across its threshold. Many stall at this point in the journey because they demand to see what is beyond the open door before they are willing to step into it.

What you need to see is not visible in the realm of natural options and solutions. Seeing with natural eyes will only cause you to stumble and stall. The way forward will appear like you are stepping into nothingness, but it will actually become a step onto something fresh and beautiful and solid.

As you step forward, you will be responding to the Voice. Listen for the Voice. The Voice is your doorway. The one who said, "I am the Door" is the Voice inviting you to step forward into a new and unfamiliar place. Once you cross this threshold and enter this doorway, you will see what was not previously visible in your current circumstance.

You Have Permission to Carry Less

You have said, "Just one more thing. I can carry just one more thing." The problem with thinking you can carry just one more thing is that at some point you will not be able to carry anything. What you need at this time in your life is to allow the wisdom of God—not the demands of other people or yourself—to determine what you carry.

This is your permission slip to carry less into the next season. Look it all over—everything you have felt you needed to carry—and ask yourself, "Did God ask me to carry all of this?" Some of the items you now carry should have been set down long ago, but you felt obligated to continue carrying them. It seems like you inherited these things, but they are not part of your inheritance.

This could be a turning point for you—a free and unencumbered departure into a place of freedom. Not everyone will understand or appreciate your decision to lighten your load. It is hard to shake hands with the new future God has planned if your hands are filled with things you are not supposed to carry. Put it all down, and only pick up one piece at a time as directed by God. Listen closely for His voice. At some point He will say, "That is enough."

So You Took the Wrong Road

In a series of less-than-perfect life decisions you ended up taking the wrong road. You made a fateful turn, and now you are miles into a regretful decision. The reality of your mistake is hitting you in the face with the full force of its implications.

At first you felt panic, but now the panic has given way to resignation. You feel like you have no other option. This fatalism is not the thinking of someone who understands they are loved, forgiven, and accepted by God.

God is not your punisher; He is your Father. He wants you to make this journey with joy. When did you start believing God has no other plan of rescue apart from letting you continue down this road of sorrow and regret?

It is never possible to go back to square one and start all over again. You would never be able find your way back through all the mistakes. God doesn't want a list of promises from you to never do this again. He knows you don't want to repeat this journey. What He wants from you is to offer Him a repentant and humble heart. Once God has your heart in His hand, He will pick you up from this painful road and put you on the road He wanted you to take in the first place. That is how a loving Father relates to His children.

Shouting Voices of Condemnation

There are times when the least informed voices speak the loudest. These loud voices, sometimes spoken with dishonor, are designed to get your attention, divert your energy, and occupy your time in personal defense.

While all the shouting is taking place, listen for God. His powerful voice will be expressed in a gentle whisper of affirmation. As condemning voices continue to speak, strain to hear the quiet whisper of God. This listening is your act of spiritual warfare.

The voices that do not know your heart will eventually pass and become distant echoes remembered only by those who have chosen to believe the worst about you.

The Power of a Moment

You are wondering how long everything will take. You wonder how long you will live—how long before love comes your way, how long before someone walks into his or her destiny, how long before your faithfulness is rewarded? You are asking "how long?" for so many things.

You only have this moment of time. This moment is a capsule you live within as you move forward through linear time. It is a vehicle that transports you through the events of life. As you arrive in your future, you will still be surrounded only by the moment. A moment is not measured in time because it is simply part of being.

Your questioning of how long all these things will take is disengaging you from the power of the moment. In this moment, you have all the authority you will ever possess. You carry with you the potential exercise of supernatural faith. The future can give you none of what you already possess. The only thing changeable is a new realization of what you carry in this moment.

Once you realize what you carry, the old questions will stop, and you will begin asking new questions. "God, what can I do in this moment?" "How can I better respond to your voice?" The answers to these questions will be where you discover the new future God has planned for your life.

Painted Into a Corner

You have painted yourself into a corner. Mistakes and misjudgments have brought you to this place. As you look out from this isolated corner, you feel like you want to break free and run, but you are afraid of ruining the paint job.

The natural mind says, "Wait until the paint is dried and then walk out. You have plenty of time to make things right." The danger with this way of thinking is that in the wait you can begin to die emotionally, and relationships could be put in jeopardy. Today, right now, stand up and begin to walk back across the wet-painted floor of the past mistakes, ignoring the mess your obedience will create.

Those who are spiritually minded will not see your paint-spotted shoes or your footprints on the floor as negative things. They will cheer you on because they see God at work in your life. The paint on your shoes and the tracks you leave behind will be a reminder to the rest of us of your willingness to do the right thing no matter what the cost. A life without these kinds of footprints is not an honest life because each life that moves deeper into the things of God will leave behind the evidence of that journey.

The Dull Blades of Criticism

Not all words cut like a sharp knife. Some words cut with the dull blade of malicious intent. The pain from these wounds is intense. The person who spoke to you did not know your heart. Their words were fueled by an ignorant anger. As a result, you have been left with a wound: a jagged and raw incision of unrighteous judgment.

Like a wound healing in the natural process of a physical body, there is a healing process in the Spirit. These wounds take time to heal. This process of healing is not because God cannot instantly heal you. God takes time to do this kind of work because He wants to use the healing process to get to the deeper place where these hurtful words matter.

That deeper place was exposed by these unloving comments. Ask God's Spirit to show you what is at the bottom of the wound channel. This will be a powerful discovery. Once you discover this buried place and disempower it with God's truth, the next time the blades of criticism and judgment begin to slash away at you, they won't land in a wound; they will land in God's truth.

What You Carry

You carry far more than you realize. The moment you were born again, God deposited His eternal and all-powerful Spirit inside your life. You have become a carrier of Presence.

You carry all the gifts of the Spirit needed to build and equip the Church. If somehow a new world was discovered and you were sent there — alone — you would carry within you everything needed to build and mature the Church in that new world. God wouldn't need to send anyone else with you because you carry the absolute fullness of God's Spirit; you have it all. "By his divine power, God has given us everything we need for living a godly life" (II Peter 1:3).

Live your life based on what you carry, not based on the fear of what you think you lack. God has made you ready to engage all aspects of life. You need nothing more than the exercise of your faith that will release the powerful presence of the One you carry.

Your Past, Your Future

Your past cannot be changed. However, your past can be redeemed. The failures of your past have been swallowed up by the new life God has given you. Allow the love of God to digest your past; otherwise, if not properly reconciled, it will become a choking bone of regret if you try to consume it by yourself.

Only God is able to reinterpret the scarring events of your past and restore what was lost. God is able to breathe new life into these dead places. He can cause a river to flow in the dry desert of personal failure. He can completely rebuild the most broken places in your past and give you a testimony of His goodness.

Because we walk by faith and not by sight, we cannot see our future with clarity. Our past is visible and loud. Our unrevealed future is silent and invisible.

As God begins this work, listen for His gentle voice, spoken in barely discernable whispers of invitation, to speak to you of the hope of a new future. Step toward the gentleness and peace of God's voice and away from the noise and confusion of your past. This is your way forward.

Author Contact Information

www.GarrisElkins.com

Garris Elkins
Prophetic Horizons
P.O. Box 509
Jacksonville, Oregon 97530